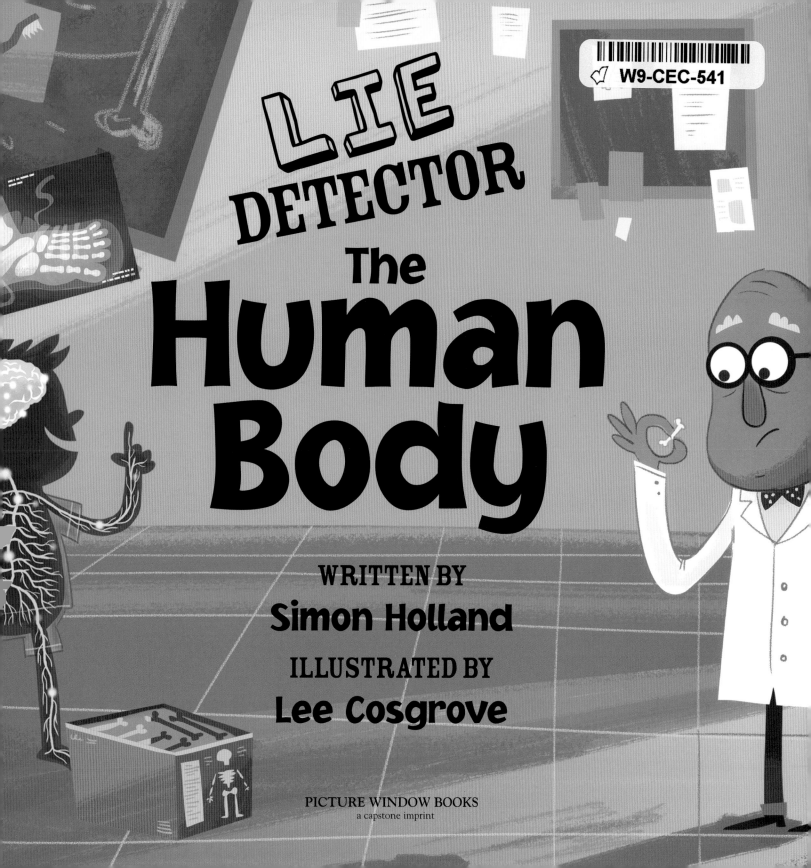

LIE
DETECTOR
The
Human
Body

WRITTEN BY
Simon Holland

ILLUSTRATED BY
Lee Cosgrove

PICTURE WINDOW BOOKS
a capstone imprint

Picture Window Books are published by
Capstone, 1710 Roe Crest Drive,
North Mankato, Minnesota 56003
www.capstonepub.com

© 2016 Weldon Owen
This edition by Picture Window Books,
a Capstone imprint.

Library of Congress
Cataloging-in-Publication Data
Cataloging-in-publication information is on file
with the Library of Congress.

ISBN 978-1-4795-8511-3 (hardcover)
ISBN 978-1-4795-8515-1 (paperback)
ISBN 978-1-4795-8519-9 (eBook PDF)

Written by Simon Holland

Printed in China
10 9 8 7 6 5 4 3 2 1

All photographs Shutterstock

LIE DETECTOR
The
Human
Body

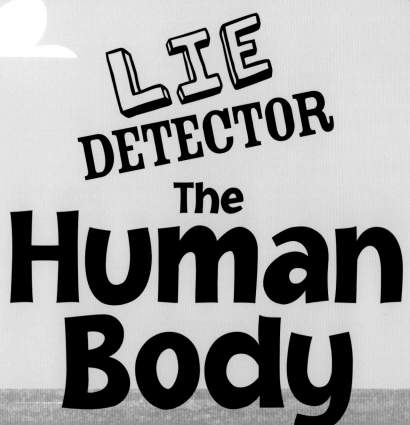

WRITTEN BY

Simon Holland

ILLUSTRATED BY

Lee Cosgrove

PICTURE WINDOW BOOKS
a capstone imprint

Do you know about the secrets under your skin? Find out, and become an expert on the human body!

When you look at the human body, you see what's happening on the outside. There are thousands of things going on inside the body too! For hundreds of years, scientists have studied the body and its systems. They have told us how the body really works.

Can you use your head to get to the bottom of the body's many mysteries? Take a look at these fact-or-fib questions to test your brain!

FACT!

DnA is a material in the body. It holds instructions for how the body will grow, develop, work, and look. As much as 99 percent of our human DNA is the same as a chimp's DNA. That's bananas!

FACT!

Water makes up more than half the weight of a human body. It carries important materials to parts of the body and gets rid of waste from organs. Water also keeps the body at the right temperature.

FIB!

A newborn baby has as many as 300 bones. As its body grows and develops, many of these bones join together. By adulthood, there are only 206 bones in the skeleton.

FACT!

The gluteus maximus is the largest muscle in the human body. It is part of a group of muscles that make up the buttocks. This big muscle helps us to stand on our two legs. It also allows us to move our hips and thighs. So get up and twirl that hula hoop!

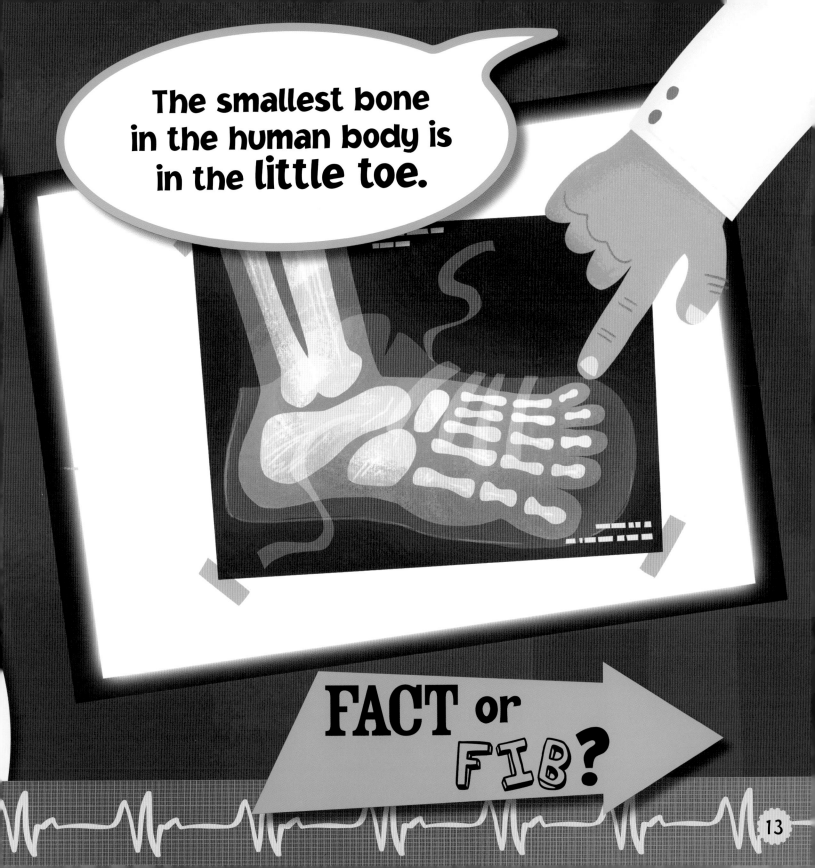

STAPES

EAR CANAL

FIB!

The smallest bone in the human body is tricky to find. That's because it's in the middle part of the ear. It's a stirrup-shaped bone called the stapes, and it's just 0.13 inches (0.33 cm) long. That's not much bigger than the nail on your little toe!

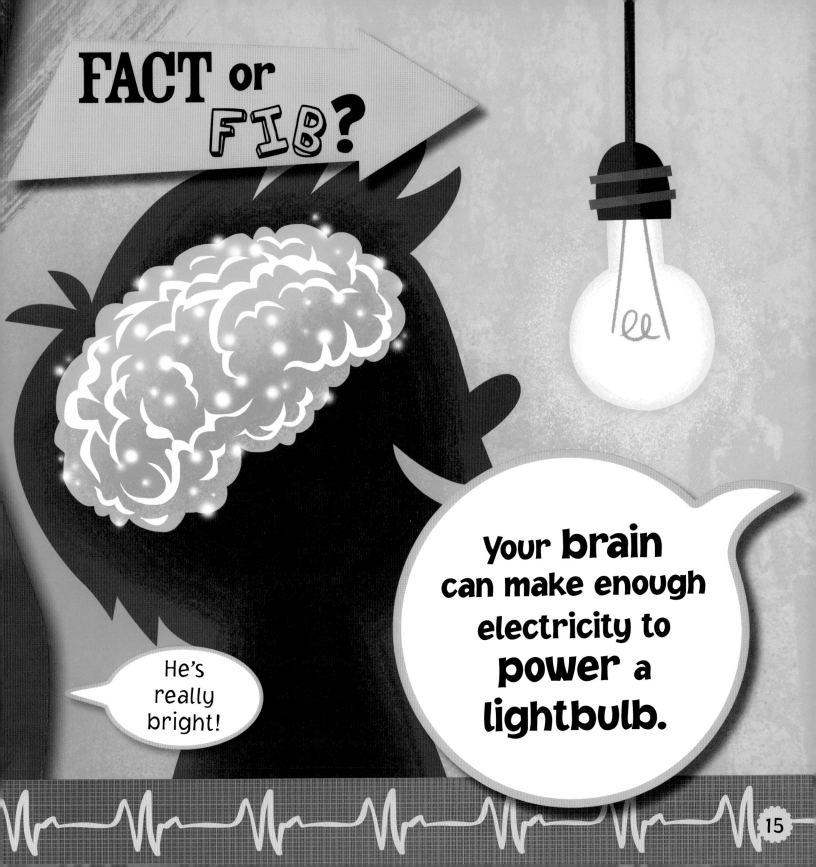

FACT!

Tiny cells called neurons carry electrical signals to the brain. Every time you move, see, think, or hear, electric signals zap around in the brain. The signals carry information to control your body. When all of these neurons work together, enough electricity is produced to power a lightbulb.

LEFT OR RIGHT?

The right side of the brain controls the left half of the body, while the left side of the brain controls the right half of the body.

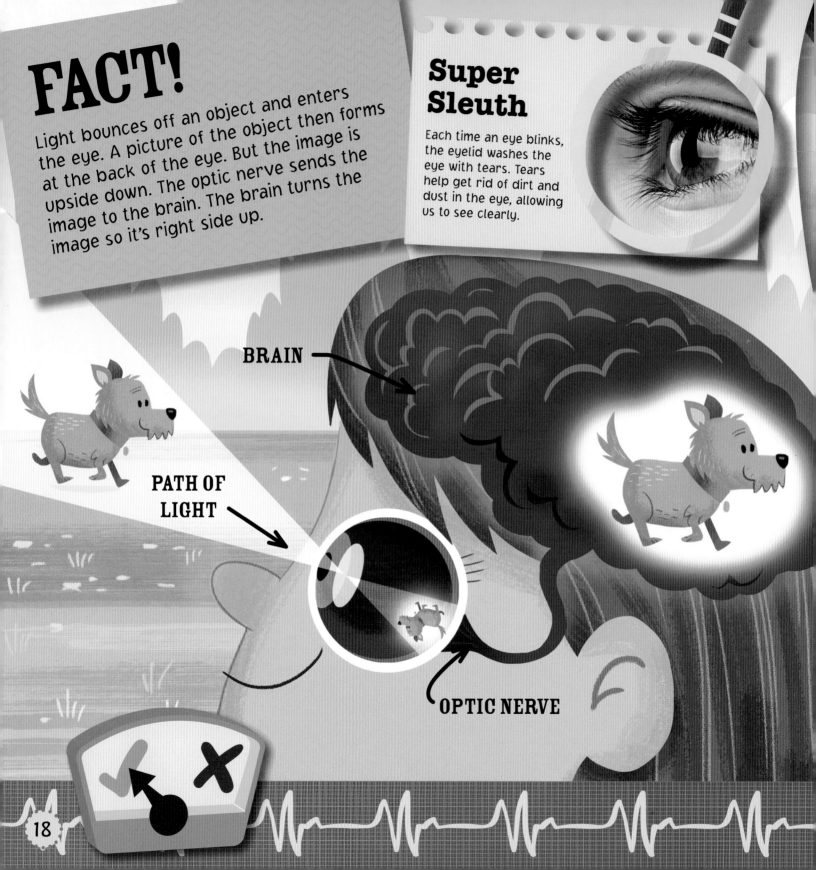

FACT!

Light bounces off an object and enters the eye. A picture of the object then forms at the back of the eye. But the image is upside down. The optic nerve sends the image to the brain. The brain turns the image so it's right side up.

Super Sleuth

Each time an eye blinks, the eyelid washes the eye with tears. Tears help get rid of dirt and dust in the eye, allowing us to see clearly.

BRAIN

PATH OF LIGHT

OPTIC NERVE

19

FACT!

Even when resting, adults breathe in and breathe out 6 quarts (5.7 liters) of air every minute. That adds up to more that 900,712 gallons (3.4 million liters) of air each year! That's more than enough air to fill an average-sized hot-air balloon!

WINDPIPE

LUNGS

GASSY GOODNESS!

The body needs oxygen to make its cells, tissues, and organs work. When we breathe in, air enters our lungs. This is where the vital oxygen gets into our blood.

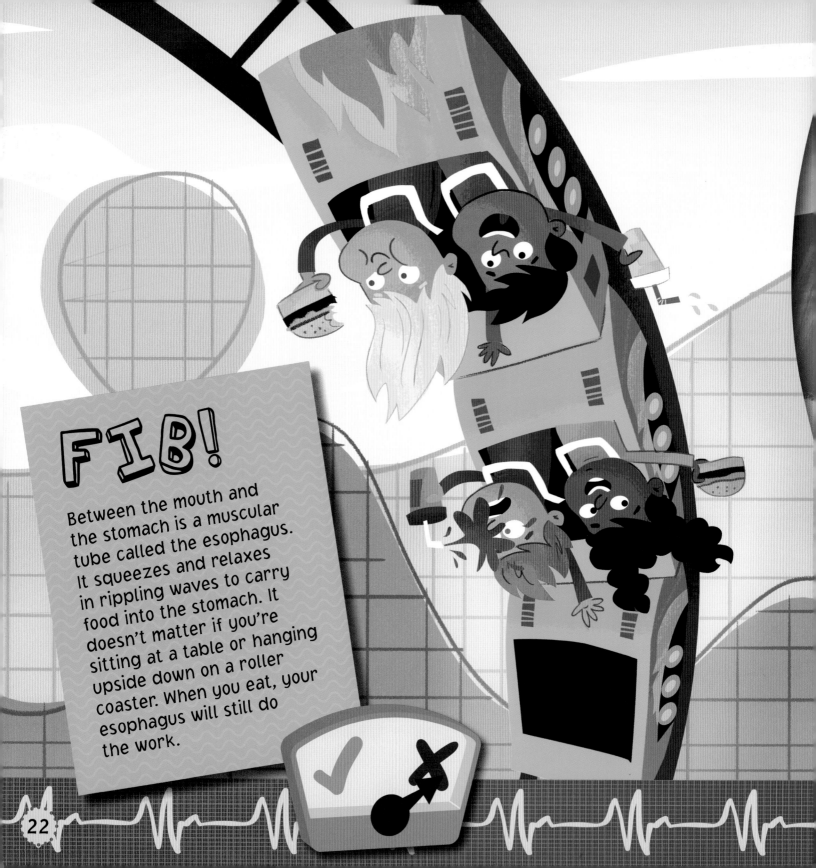

FIB!

Between the mouth and the stomach is a muscular tube called the esophagus. It squeezes and relaxes in rippling waves to carry food into the stomach. It doesn't matter if you're sitting at a table or hanging upside down on a roller coaster. When you eat, your esophagus will still do the work.

YOUR TEETH

FIB!

Sharks lose their teeth and grow new ones throughout their lives! Humans aren't quite so lucky. Infants grow baby teeth. As the child grows, the baby teeth fall out to make room for adult teeth. Most people have 32 adult teeth. If an adult tooth falls out, no new tooth will grow.

Super Sleuth

Humans have four main kinds of teeth. Sharp teeth cut and pointed teeth tear food. Flat teeth chew, and our back teeth grind food.

STOP THE CLOCK

It takes about one minute for a single blood cell to zoom all the way around the body.

FIB!

Actually, it's even more! After 70 years the average heart will have pumped about 49 million gallons (185 million liters) of blood around the body. An Olympic-sized swimming pool can hold about 650,000 gallons of liquid. So, a human heart could fill at least 75 pools over the course of an average lifetime.

HEART PUMPS OUT THE BLOOD

BLOOD FILLS THE HEART

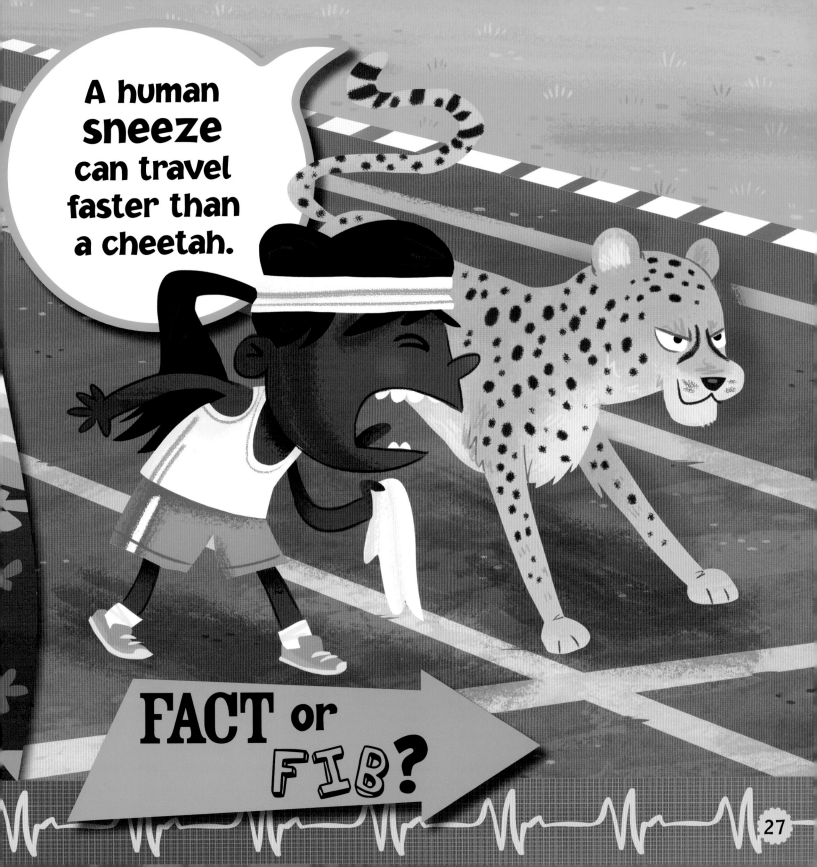

FACT!

The cheetah is the world's fastest animal. It can run at least 62 miles (100 kilometers) per hour. But a cheetah is totally out-sprinted by your snot! A sneeze can travel at about 68 miles (109 km) per hour. Just look at it go!

Be good to yourself ...

So, what have you learned from this fun-filled tour of the human body? You now know that you're similar to a chimp and your body is made mostly of water. You also discovered your muscular bottom helps you move around on your legs. And most importantly, you found out that your snot would beat a cheetah in a race! On the next page there's one final challenge for you.

GUESS WHAT?

Scientists and doctors use special equipment to see inside the body. X-rays help us see hard materials, such as bones, in the body. Special scans that use x-rays and a computer show us images of our innards. These tools help us find health problems that may exist. See if you can match these close-up pictures to the correct parts of the human body.

2. What do bones combine to make?

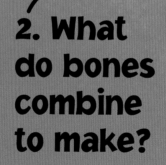

1. Which organs take oxygen from the air?

3. Can you name the body's control center?

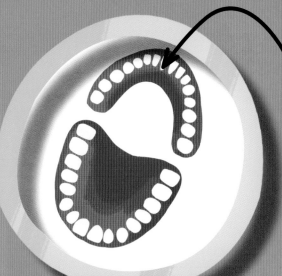

4. What grows in when you lose baby teeth?

5. Where are these tiny little bones found?

CHOOSE YOUR ANSWERS FROM THESE BODY PARTS:

A. Brain
B. Middle ear
C. Adult teeth
D. Lungs
E. Skeleton

GLOSSARY

bone—bones are lengths of hard, whitish tissue that make up the body's framework, the skeleton

cell—cells are tiny building blocks that make up all living things

DNA— material in cells that carries all of the instructions to make a living thing and keep it working

muscle—a tissue in the body that is made of strong fibers; muscles can be tightened or relaxed to make the body move

neuron—a tiny cell that helps to pass nerve signals around the body

optic nerve—a tiny fiber that sends messages from the eye to the brain

organ—a body part that does a certain job. The heart, lungs, and skin are all organs

oxygen—a gas that we take in through breathing to help our cells make energy and do their jobs in the body

tissue—a layer or bunch of soft material that makes up body parts

INDEX